POETRY
now

CLOUDBURST

Edited by

Zoë Rock

First published in Great Britain in 2001 by
POETRY NOW
Remus House,
Coltsfoot Drive,
Peterborough, PE2 9JX
Telephone (01733) 898101
Fax (01733) 313524

HB ISBN 0 75432 688 8
SB ISBN 0 75432 689 6

FOREWORD

Although we are a nation of poets we are accused of not reading poetry, or buying poetry books. After many years of listening to the incessant gripes of poetry publishers, I can only assume that the books they publish, in general, are books that most people do not want to read.

Poetry should not be obscure, introverted, and as cryptic as a crossword puzzle: it is the poet's duty to reach out and embrace the world.

The world owes the poet nothing and we should not be expected to dig and delve into a rambling discourse searching for some inner meaning.

The reason we write poetry (and almost all of us do) is because we want to communicate: an ideal; an idea; or a specific feeling. Poetry is as essential in communication, as a letter; a radio; a telephone, and the main criterion for selecting the poems in this anthology is very simple: they communicate.

Contents

Triggered La Trigg

It was once only fantasy
which became reality,
short-lived,
chaotic,
alive.

Even now as sleep creeps,
my mind becomes steeped
and I drift back,
seduced by those times.

With burning toxicity
comes warping images,
of conversations rehearsed,
reversed.

Then the memory's stilled,
and I'm back on those hills
where my soulmate waits,
'Don't leave it too late.'

Take me back,
take me back to home.

Amy Phillips

Field Of Dreams

Around my field of dreams, there is no fence,
My thoughts and dreams, to me make sense,
Within my field of dreams, there is only peace,
In my field of dreams, I can open my mind
And forget all those thoughts that bind,
In my field of dreams, I dream only of pleasure,
And pass the time away at my leisure,
In my field of dreams, happiness is all around,
And only soft voices and music sound,
In my field of dreams, I can soundly sleep,
And all my secrets and thoughts I can keep,
But all too soon, consciousness will descend,
And my field of dreams will fade then come to an end.

Allan John Young

Blue Anchor Bay

Talked we of ifs'
And memories
Upon those cliffs,
In fields and trees.
You sigh to me,
You happy day
Blue sky, blue sea
Blue Anchor Bay.

Roger Mosedale

A Place Of Dreams

Connemara lonely spot
The peat-bog stillness smoothly green,
Relaxing, sloping to the sea,
A lovely vista, to be seen.

Away from all the traffic noise,
In beauty, just the place to dream,
With just a solitary bird,
Strutting beside a silver stream.

A gentle wind, a hint of rain,
When scudding clouds obscure the sun,
Just you and I to share the peace,
Just two - away from everyone.

Leonard T Coleman

A Perfect Place

There is a place on this green earth
That I have grown to love,
Pastures filled with summer mirth
That mirror the sky above.

Bluebells shimmer in the shade,
Where the grass stands tall and green,
Hint of glory that will never fade,
And a serenity seldom seen.

It is a place where dreamers wander
To watch the setting of the sun,
At nature's majesty they can only ponder
When the day is nearly done.

For I have felt the bitter chills
That come in many forms,
But there is no sweeter sight than those green hills;
My summer in life's winter storms.

And of all the places I could roam,
The places where I could dwell,
There are none so perfect as the sight of home;
And the land I know so well.

Rebecca Osborne

My Dream

If only I could win just once
A million pounds would do
I'd buy a nice big house for me
And a caravan for you

It's not that I am selfish
Nor wish to make you suffer
I want to make my life complete
And yours a little rougher

No longer would I be your slave
Do your washing, make your grub
If you want to get your meals on time
Then you can get them down the pub

It's not that I do bear a grudge
Nor wish you any harm
It's just that you are lacking
In a share of gentlemanly charm

I think I'd find myself a man
Who was handsome and divine
We'd live happily together
In this unlikely dream of mine

So until my numbers all come up
And I win the lottery pot
I suppose I must be satisfied
With the man that I have got.

Pat Stott

LIVING ROOM HORROR

The room was very dark,
Its light restricted by
A hard, concrete shelter,
Courtesy of the war.

Wireless, with much cable!
Spilling news over folk;
Alvar Liddel telling
What must surely be lies.

At least, the child huddled
On the dim stairs thinks so.
Nasty, bad stories.
People wouldn't do that.

The name came much later,
'Holocaust'. New, sad word
Did not explain the pains
Or give the child a reason.

Joan Kelly

Springtime Woman

Today was a glorious, gleeful spring in step
with the snow's retreat and framed in heat,
the daffodils and tulips sprang afresh
even littered on the street (I picked them up
of course and held them gentle, held them caring)
whilst yearling birds unearthed their food and hid
behind the scarcely budded wood of pruned bush
and stripling tree and I noticed every slip of green,
every sparkling aconite, every speedwell,
every tuft of newly spangled grass, where
ice had melted and the green of this bright
new year had shown its all. Before the stamp
of boots in Sunday's game, the walking dogs,
the wintered pony with its moulting mane
and flywisk tail, the munch of earthworms
in the bank, the reaping council's grim faced mowerman,
all take their toll, before even the vandals have
broken trail, early in the morning light I saw
the glorious gleeful spring, echoed in my step
(Last night I had a phone call).
Running almost, weighted down, yet spring eternal spring
was born. (Today I hold your card close to my heart)
Wearing spring green, feeling sunny, thoughts of you
and suddenly, I noticed every sign of spring.

Lesley Vann

A PLACE OF DREAMS

I dream of . . .?
A shady nook?
A bubbling stream?
A soaring peak?
A blissful shore?
In my youth.
Not now.
No more.
Idealism
Seeped into reality
Long since.
Now
I dream of justice,
Care, equality
And peace.
But it's only a dream.
Not real,
And not a place at all.

Ann Bryce

My Cornish Retreat

July stirs my memory
Of where I used to stay
In a little Cornish village
By the sea.

No popcorn or rock,
Sold in my retreat,
Just Cornish pasties
I loved to eat.

I stayed in a bungalow
On the side of a hill
Looking down on the sand
And the sea.
Little boats in the distance
Completed the picture for me.

Irene Millington

FROM STALAG IVB 1944

As I stood and gazed at the evening's close,
All around me there arose,
The queer shaped stacks of that busy town,
Chimney on chimney bottles brown,
Up amid the blue-black tiles,
Away across for miles and miles,
And from them belched a man-made cloud,
Clothing the city in its shroud,
And as upon its way it rolled,
Nature tinted it with gold,
Then suddenly a glare of red,
Rising from an open bed,
Of molten steel, soon to be,
Shining and living machinery,
Lit it up, like a glimpse of Hell,
Rolling fire, that on each swell,
Twisted and turned, so to me giving,
The thought that it might too be living,
Whereon my mind evolved a form,
Like a ghostly spectre from a storm,
Grimacing, beckoning, where e'er I went,
Back to my home in the vale of Trent,
That place o'er which the smoke is curled,
Yet spreads its beauty throughout the world.

Joe Holloway

MORNING IDYLL

Cool, pale light, low-angled
Along thickets and hedges,
Haloes seeds of wild clematis;
Transforming them into luminous,
Fragile blossoms of thistle-down.

Gossamer threads, bespangled,
With droplets, quiver from branch
To bare branch, pin-pointing with
Pellucid clarity, speared darts
Of brilliant, prismatic colours;

While in small pools, bangled
Rings of sparkling crystal
Form, where glinting spherules
Drop and splinter the surface
Of their smooth, mirror faces;

And through the long, tangled
Tresses of the drooping willow,
The eye dew-fresh from sleep,
Absorbs the scintillating beauty,
Of this shining jewel of a day.

Bronwen Gould

My Love

How I wish you were here beside me,
in this paradise by the sea.
It's all we ever wished for -
in fact it's so much more!
The sky is blue and cloudless,
with a sun that shines regardless.
The azure sea, such a beautiful blue,
laps gently to the sand giving such a wonderful view.
Palm trees wave gently in the breeze,
flowers have such delicate beauty, their fragrance doth me please.
Shells of every shape and size, scattered on the shore,
remembering how you love them makes me miss you more.
Stones and rocks abounding make me chuckle so,
as I remember the struggles you had with them in time past as
homeward we did go!
The fruit and nuts that grow here are lovely as can be,
somehow I can't bring myself to cook the animals for tea . . .
I love to watch them playing, because you see,
they have no inhibitions, they are completely oblivious to me!
It's the nights that are the hardest I find,
when memories flit through my mind.
So many times we dreamed of sleeping beneath the stars,
well here am I and here are they - but you might as well be on Mars!
I miss your touch so tender,
your smile, your red gold curls through which my fingers love
to meander.
Your shoulders broad and arms to hold me close,
the sweep of your lashes on your cheek in repose.
We both know we are soulmates,
created and brought together by God, not the 'fates'.
So goodnight my love, God bless you,
- please come and be my rescue!

Margi Hughes

Dreams

The thing I like about dreams
Is how comforting they seem
They may not be realistic
But keep us optimistic
They can keep us safe at night
And they scare away the fright.

They cannot be right or wrong
They're something that keeps you strong
They strengthen the will to cope
And can even give us hope
They give us an aim in life
When our problems give us strife.

When there's a space that once was full
They help to give us a pull
When our loved ones let us down
They can chase away the frown
When abandoned and bereft,
Dreams are all that we have left.

That's what I like about dreams.

Amy Thomas (17)

ETERNAL

You are a burning fire
of Hope
You are the stalwart
of a forgotten race

You are the ensign
of humanity

To you I seek
for sweet embrace

You are my life
in another kingdom
You are my incarnate
my guiding star

You are my lover
my destiny leads me

To always be near
wherever you are

There is a mystery
sweet mystery in Heaven
There is an infinite
we're infinite too

You are my lover
who calls when he needs me

Always - Forever
I'll be there with you.

Mary Skelton

LOMOND

By the banks of Lomond
there's where my rainbow ends,
amidst the mists on banks and brae's
tranquillity descends;
the shimmer ore' the waters
cascading down the streams,
to end my days in beauty such
would answer all my dreams.
To gaze from lofty mountain tops
or 'neath the fir and bracken,
for me dear Loch in memory
your beauty ever beckons;
'come away - return to me'
like pipes within my heart -
forever more there'll always be
that 'Stirling' in my heart;
return to you - be sure I will
when God and time allow,
in heart - in mind - in memory
Aye I am wi ye still.

Barbara Petrow

My Place Of Dreams

My place of dreams will always be
A little island across the sea,
A place where great tall palm trees grow,
To shade me from the bright sun's glow.

A little place with a sandy beach,
Where we could sit and laze all day,
Enjoying the peace and tranquillity
Which makes all your cares float away.

But would we really be happy,
With nothing to do all day,
Or would we long for the home we had left,
In our homeland across the sea.

For the beauty we find on an island,
We can find in our back yard,
The flowers bloom, and the trees grow tall,
Our own loving care brings its own reward.

A dream is just a dream,
No need far away to roam,
For happiness is where the heart is,
In our own little home sweet home.

Iris Covell

A New Hope

The emerald lay shining bare,
Through the darkened windows misted,
And all the power glowing there
Gouged the ground and trees twisted.

This is earth's only remaining prize.
The energy ephemeral forever flowing.
The only thing it still likes to guise,
To keep the grass and forest growing.

But not a sole sapling saw
The being that, like the horse of Troy,
Entered in peace, during the heart of war,
And did at night the emerald destroy.

By boldly breaking the bright green gem,
He'd plucked the flower from its stem.
Yet the remnants and shatters of it seem
To still through those misted windows beam.

The sustenance absorbed from its internal power
Enough for the rebirth of a phoenix flower.
And from the shards of its initial grave
Begin the fetch of earth's next great wave.

R McGinty

ODE ON AN OPERATION

Recumbent, gazing ever to the sky
Transported to a theatre full of light
Along wide corridors, I ask not why
But breathe more deeply, stranger to the sight.

With just a silent sigh, let eyelids droop
The lifeless air, the sleepy tranquil place
Hypnotic draught leads on to slumber's stoop
Pain killing panacea - as swirls of silken lace

A place of dreams, of fantasies and fears
Of space and secrets, solitude, so free
Where no-one can intrude; a thousand years
A single second filled with destiny.

Then misty swirling lights appear to shine
And green cloaked people's voice in anxious tone
'It's over now' and yet I still recline
Unaccompanied, yet not alone.

The theatre staff remove their mask, I moan.
So wide and long the corridor still seems.
Those secret fantasies, once vivid, now have flown
And all I know, 'twas just *a place of dreams.*

Gerald S Bell

Dreamtime

We had battled through The Forests to glimpse the Brighter Day,
and as we broke out from the Shadows, so the Darkness slipped away.
We stood silent at The Crossroads, as we beheld The Shafts of Dawn,
shining on The Swirl of Eden to Create a Brave New Morn.
As The Sun gave forth its Glory and The Banners so unfurled
The Vision slowly opened all throughout The World.

And gone were all The Ravages that used to haunt The World
and I wondered of The Mysteries that thus around me swirled.
Am I a traveller lost in time? Adrift in ages past,
or is this 'The Happy Hunting Ground' or maybe Paradise at last.

And I saluted to my Brothers, who on hoof came passing by.
And I gazed towards my Cousins soaring gently through the sky.
And I called out to the Wolves, who had returned once more
and out on the rolling grasslands, there roamed Buffalo and Wild Boar.

Then a Warrior on a White Horse sped towards me, riding fast.
Was this a forgotten enemy - from a battle long time past?
But as The Rider neared me, I beheld features quite sublime
and he spoke of Prophecy and Portent and of The Mysteries of Time . . .

'Behold, thee now these wonders,
That are thus throughout this land,
These are coming, yet these have gone,
Yet these now before thee stand.
Believe me when I tell thee,
This is a world within thy grasp,
And what ye yearn and what ye seek,
Will surely come to pass.
Ye may find what ye so yearn,
When ye ride both right and true,
So dream hard and ride on fearlessly.
Ye have glimpsed the old and new'

And so we travelled on back to The Crossroads,
Where we paused for a while at the bend,
And as we returned through The Forests of Darkness,
The Vision rode alongside as A Friend.

John Martindale

My Eternity

There is a place where there is no more sorrow, crying and pain.
There is a place where there is happiness, laughter and joy.
There is an everlasting light, there is no darkness.
Sickness and disease is banished.
Poverty and anxiety is no more.
Love reigns forever.
There is constant singing, beautiful melodies fill the air.
There are amazing parties all day and every day.
Everything dances in praise to its Creator.
This is the place I long to go.
The place I will one day call home.
Where my friends and family will all be reunited.
This is my heaven, my paradise, my eternity.

Samantha Drewry

Dream Cottage

A cottage in the country with roof of golden thatch,
With roses round the door and a brilliant flower patch,
The gurgling stream beside flowing straight into the pond,
Covered with water lilies and all aquatic plants
An array of koi and goldfish in the depths beyond,
A dancing fountain and a waterfall
To sit by and relax, in summertime ahead.

A warm and cosy cottage as winter comes along,
The fire burning merrily in the grate -
With the logs piled up on the side,
Weather cold and crisp and the children love to slide,
The snow is coming down and snowmen all made
Christmas round the corner, the smell of cooking
through the house,
My dream cottage at the top of my list.

V Harding

OUR SECRET PLACE

To reach the place we called our own
We walked with determination . . .
To a cove, where we seemed all alone,
No need for conversation.

Flat rocks eroded by the sea,
These were our chairs and table,
A spot each year we went to see . . .
Whenever we were able.

Such peace was there, no one intruded,
'Our' special world private, secluded.
If the sea was calm, only birds would pass . . .
Over tiny rock pools smooth as glass.

But when the tide came flowing to the shore . . .
The mighty waves made a loud and crashing roar,
Through crevices like a fountain high
Midst the eerie sound of the sea birds cry.

Spectacular like glistening rain . . .
Cascading back to earth again.
What power and what majesty,
The glories of earth, sky and sea.

I know for us those times are past,
But memories in my mind will last.
I hope some day, somewhere, again we'll meet . . .
To visit once again our lovely, lost, retreat.

Joan Carr

To: 'B'

Huddled in the doorway of a most imposing shop,
I sheltered from the biting wind and rain.
But still I was despondent; the shiv'ring did not stop -
Here in my 'haven', so what had I to gain?
I wandered into 'Travelroom', saw countless shelves and stands
Full of glossy brochures for each 'dot' upon the globe.
'Southern Africa', a copy fell into my hands
Dream-filled views of wildlife and a splendid Zulu robe.

My mind takes flight 'til it comes to rest
Allured, beneath the African sky.
So awesome the landscape it gives a zest
To venture far - watch great birds fly.
Just step on board the train called 'Blue'
In sumptuous style, come, wine and dine.
On Rovos Rail, times past and new
Perfect in elegance, do combine.
Traverse the bush - be 'stunned' on safari -
The 'Big Five' impact the sight and sense.
Now the mood changes - here vibrant city
Participation - a feeling intense.
Oh! Wondrous nature - Victoria Falls.
Seek solace in beauteous sunset.
Climb Table Mountain - but the cable car 'calls' . . .
Penguins. See penguins! My deepest joy yet.

Voices break through my reverie -
I catch the words 'intend' and 'spend'.
I drift back to my fantasy -
This place I share - with my dream friend.

Beryl Mapperley

DAYDREAM DOMAIN

Adventures happen every day -
Go deeper, submerge, explore.
Discover the tricks
In every box of minutes!

Take one sunny eternity to behold, to smile,
Here, in line, with Rangitoto Isle.
Enthral in interpreting the soul's window
Of views over mighty landscapes.
Keep the minutes you breathe!

Take again, inhale the down and yawn
Gulfs of this camomile lawn.
Tumble in odiforous clouds of herb
Fluffing your travels in time.
Feel the minutes you breathe!

Go guided by pohtukawa lights,
Red hot constellations across the night.
Red, red like nothing ever was,
Blood flows pink in this truest colour.
See the minutes you breathe!

Adventures happen every day for us -
Keep each time it's awful thunder,
Lest you litter your lives and epitaphs
With blind and lifeless days of wonder.

Nicholas Daniels

A Road To Dreams

Dear Reader,

Allow me to take you onto a road, a road into a land far distant and wide. 'Tis a road but a dream where trees are made from rich dairy cream. In butterscotch fields where brilliant splashes of custard cups of daffodils, bow to the fairies upon Angel Delight hills.

From underneath vanilla toadstools munchkins gobble noisily bacon and ham crisps of leaves near to strawberry roses caviar pastures lie still while goblins from champagne rivers quench their fill. Fizzy psychedelic coloured rainbows arch over turquoise skies where cottonwool velvet clouds smile on by.

Orange and pink pumpkins busily devour dark chocolate tasty flies mischievous pixies taunt trolls hidden beneath tantalised sherbert mushrooms with such harks of marshmellow sighs. Forest floors laid mired in Turkish Delight liquor give growth to peppermint shrubs while busy toffee ants smell the aroma of pork beef twigs so pure. Whence pumpkins dance beneath sunset skies on an ocean of cranberry honey. Yet far in a corner the Fairy Queen points to an alighted door glazed in rich hazelnut cream. 'Tis where the little folk will guide you dear reader should you want to enter their road to dream . . .

Diane Full

ENTRANCE TO THE CRYSTAL CAVE

Following in the footprints,
That lie before us,
Across the stretch of warm white sand,
As the hazy sun overhead,
Gently beats down,
We reach the shoreline,

The frothy white gently lapping waves,
Splash across our toes,
Settling in the imprints,
We leave behind,
As we survey the turquoise ocean,
And far into the distance,

Our thoughts still,
Until we become as one,
With the vast expanse of water,
Merging with its mighty rushing sound,
And its power as it gathers,
Momentum in each wave,

The seagull riding on the therm,
Calls out as it swoops and dives,
Low across the sea,
Soon we reach a small cove,
A paradise where we linger a short while,
The footprints from here divert inland,

Grains of sand push between our toes,
Until we eventually come to an outcrop of rocks,
Carefully climbing up,
We feel the roughness of the granite,
Upon the soles of our feet,
We then find a small hidden entrance,

Crouching, we manage to crawl inside,
It takes our eyes a while to get used to the dark,
And it smells musty and feels damp,
Once more we can stand upright,
We follow a long tunnel,
Eventually seeing light towards the end,

It opens out into a large cave,
Comprised solely of the most beautiful crystals,
Walls of rose pink quartz,
Interlaced with Amethyst points,
Like the finest crystal chandeliers,
With deep purple droppers,

Jagged amber coloured Citrine,
Lying like some stately crown long since forgotten,
The centre piece a crystal quartz monolith,
Which cascades rainbow colours from its prisms,
As the shafts of sunlight filter in,
We stand in awe soaking in the energy from this life force,

Until once more we step outside into the light of day,
To follow the footprints as they lead across the sand,
We make our way down to the water's edge,
Feeling the welcome splash of the surf at our ankles,
Until we immerse completely to be at one,
With all the elements of nature and emerge refreshed.

Ann G Wallace

SUMMER DREAM

As I look out,
To the lamp post opposite,
Feeling sleepy and relaxed,
I drift back to the Greek sunset.

While sitting by the sea edge,
Still feeling the warm air,
Still hearing the soothing waves lash,
Onto the golden stretch of sand.

Bliss!

Closing one's eyes,
And the memories flow free,
Warming one's soul.

Back home to reality,
Holiday was nice while it lasted . . .
Summer dream.

Kim Rands

In Realms Victorious

Heaven reigns, Heaven victorious
The dwelling place of God, so holy, so glorious
Heaven the blessed home of the soul
Where once sinners, Amen, shall and do dwell
Made by Christ's blood, entirely whole
Heaven the home, that stands still supreme
Where love, joy and peace, is no mere empty hope,
Or dream
Where Angels stand, and a heavenly choir sing
Especially for us, as we will one day, surely sing
That forever gone, is death's sting
Yes! Heaven the place, where golden bells ring
And harps are heard,
And pure happiness bring, to the hearers
There in Heaven, God's dwelling place
So victorious, further to come proof, and by God's
Good grace, that Heaven is no dream, Praise Jesus.

Margaret Lightbody

A Wondrous Place

In the middle of a forest
Where the trees grow
Straight and tall,
And the grass is
Decked with bluebells
And the sun shines
On them all.
Where the butterflies
Go bobbing from,
Each blue and silver bell,
Settles on each flower of beauty
In this shady - peaceful Dell.
Far away a sound of music
Birds a-singing, sweet and long,
Echoing among the treetops
Sounds of rapture in their song.
Telling all to stop and listen
As they sing their roun-de la,
'Tis their hymn of praise to Heaven
As they show us how to pray.

J Winwood

VISION OF THE NIGHT

I blink,
Dragons fly bravely through a crimson sky,
Golden beaches edge out thick purple forests taller than me.
Breath is caught in bubbles solid through use.
Tomorrow never comes, only lasting memories survive the dead
heat of thirst.

I blink,
Now the crystal blue sun illuminates the rounded shoulders of lovers.
Flowing deep ocean blue dress merges seamlessly with jet black hair.
Soft lullabies cushion my sweet talk of love,
Night lost in meaningful words and open-hearted hazel eyes.

I blink,
Thunder drowns any colour as the strength of nature unfurls,
Squares of pink hid in the peal of controlling grey.
Sparks the white of angel's wings play touch on a frozen world,
Tiny raindrops fall like elephants stampeding.

I blink,
Fresh coffee fills my head with warm Sunday mornings,
French toast drips from an overflowing plate.
Happy chatter explodes from the far side of a paper mountain.
Cut glass smiles wake my morning idleness.

I blink,
Screams of frightened children shatter an unnatural silence.
Char grilled rubble act as beacons solidifying the unreal,
My shouts end deadened against limp bodies.
The tears are the only markers to the horror of human arrogance.

Ian Fisher

My Dream Island

As I closed my eyes to shut out the light, there was not a soul to
be seen,
water lapped around my feet and legs, this was like paradise from
a dream.
Beautiful odours drifting thro' the air, the ebbing waters cover my toes,
what a wonderful way to be far away, on an island that nobody knows.

It's all coming clear I have nothing to fear, there's not a cannibal
in sight,
there are dancing girls in skimpy grass skirts, 'Oh I do fancy her on the right.' I gave her a smile and she smiled back, her hips swayed with majestic ease, my pulse is racing and I'm in a sweat, she certainly knows how to tease.

I am sure the tide is coming in, the water's risen way above my thighs, 'Oh my God she's coming towards me,' I must look longingly into her eyes, I'll serenade her with that old Aker Bilk number, 'The Stranger on the Shore!'
'You won't' said the wife, 'your bath's over run; so now you can dry up the floor.'

Wenn - The - Penn

Soaring With Seagulls

I sit on high chalk cliffs
Gazing seawards into the mists of distance,
My fingers pluck at the short close packed grasses,
My mind, is gliding with seagulls!

Appreciating their ability to be remote,
As with outstretched wings they take advantage,
Floating gracefully, on the upthrust air
That rises warmly above the face of the cliff.

There is an air of relaxation, comfort,
And a feeling about this place,
Satisfaction, acceptance and appreciation,
It provides a feeling of fulfilment!

The fascinating cries of the various seabirds,
The sounds of the sea, its waves,
Of never-ending movements, it ebbs and flows,
As backwards and forwards it swells, to and fro.

The air is still and clean,
The sky is blue and clear
No sign of any impending storm,
Just a faint breeze, that is comfortably warm.

I allow myself to relax,
To revel in this calm,
Wrapped in natures natural balm,
I applaud this day, for it brings no harm!

Bah Kaffir

A SPECIAL DREAM

There is a special kind of dream
A dream to aspire!
With hope for the future,
To make life less dire.

Perhaps wish for a child
Of ones very own blood,
To bring up and cherish,
And do all that one could.

Maybe to go to a restaurant,
With plenty of cash,
And order finest cuisine,
Not 'bangers and mash'
To go on a cruise,
And sail the seven seas,
Just sit around the pool
And enjoy the sea breeze!

Some go on the lottery
And use special dates,
With visions of millions,
And posher new mates.

There is one thing to remember
Whatever your wealth,
You can't buy God's blessing,
And happiness and health.

Edith Antrobus

My Dreams, My Rainbow

We have our dreams, you and I
Looking high up to the sky
You're happy, I know with your routine lives
It's not for me, my heart it cries

I yearn for something, yet I'm still unsure
If there was just one thing, maybe then I'd know
The happiness you have, that I still seek
When you gleam with heart-filled smiles, at the beginning of each week

Some may laugh, some may not
My mind says go . . . go to find my pot
Of gold that is, at the end of my rainbow
Just to find my space, where I might grow

There'll be times that are good, there'll be times that are bad
Sometimes I'll be happy, sometimes I'll be sad
But the book I will write from beginning to end
I'll tell my story, with only my rules to bend

And if I return, will you recognise who I am
I'll have changed you see, and become more of a man
I don't know when and I don't know how long
Still I know when I return I'll be singing my song.

Dawna-Mechelle

MAGICAL MOMENTS

Over the green hills and the valleys
Over the meadows and the dales
My heart, a lamb, prances and sallies,
My vision, a vessel, spreads its sails.

Beyond the horizon a red sun is sinking,
Birds take to flight, joy on the wing.
O Lord what a glory, it sets me a-thinking
Life is a jewel, an invaluable thing.

Peace is a whisper, the breeze so uplifting,
The hush of the evening, blessed, serene,
The scent of the blossoms wafted and drifting,
The balm of the dusk descends on the scene.

Give me a voice to sing out Thy praises,
Give me a tune to dance to the stars,
Thy mantle of beauty all fretting erases
And Nature, great healer, effaces my scars.

In the distance a bell longingly chimes,
Trees decked in leaves, friendly and wise,
Lend us the beauty of mystical rhymes,
Wake up my soul and reach to the skies.

La Vigne Community, France
28th July 1988

Emmanuel Petrakis

WHERE BUZZARDS FLY

My land of dreams is not in foreign lands -
Not for me the golden sand on a sun-drenched shore
With a turquoise sea lapping gently at my feet,
Where coconut-hung palm trees nod in the scented breeze,
And the nights are cool, the air is soft
And the silver sea shimmers in the full moon's light.

But give me the bracken covered Moor,
With the tors rising all around,
Their granite boulders tumbled down the slopes.
Where buzzards mew and wheel above
And skylarks rise and sing in the clean moorland air.
Bees buzz amongst the coconut-scented gorse
Flying from flower to golden flower in the warm sun,
And rivers splash and laugh as they flow towards the sea
Under the ancient bridges that span them on their way.
Here the nights are dark, and mysterious shadows
Move across the moor under the full moon,
As it rises behind Hound Tor on an autumn night.

This is my land of dreams - this wild and ancient place.
This precious piece of England where tors and valleys,
Farm and moor live side by side in harmony.
Where time is unimportant and I can stand alone
And be surrounded by tranquillity and peace.
The past, present and future that is Dartmoor.

Ann Linney

AT THE END OF THE DAY

These are the places that define a perfect moment in time
Maybe a beach, a café or a cool, sunlit country garden
Something memorable connects them all, just as in rhyme
Valued not for material treasures, but memories they hold

A rural setting in a country park of considerable prestige
Swallows glide through the air with the greatest of ease
Children's laughter carries majestically on the breeze
The picnic hamper's empty now, time to rest, time to relax

A local eleven take to the field resplendent in white
Then a sound of crashing willow, the ball's over the line
All out, a mere ninety-seven although they put up a fight
Tea and biscuits are taken and the evening draws on

The sky once blue is now filled with an orange hue
Still a faint trace of warmth at the end of the day
The summer sun surrenders and descends gracefully
Fading just like a camp fire's last glowing embers

The tall grass meadow witnesses its gracious decline
A dead elm confidently strangles the prominent horizon
Yelping skinny dippers cautiously test the lapping water
Confident their modesty will at least be partly obscured

The transition is a smooth blend from day to night
Escher's artwork portrays it oh so completely right
At the Lake the quality of light plays and flickers
Water shimmers reflecting the moon's desolate gaze

We've all been to this place at least once in our lives
The scene induces a sense of excitement and delight
It takes on a different guise for each individual's eyes
It's where your most treasured vivid memories hide.

Neil F Poyner

SARK IN SUMMER

Hot gold flowers, rocks with fire glinted
Purple heather, sea and sky deep tinted
Spreading, meeting, blazing forth together
In a scene of mesmerising colour.

Sounds were muted - whispering waves legato
Insects droning, birdsong pizzicato
Shapes were rounded, smooth rocks lined the reaches
Curving bays and ripples, untrod beaches

Not a hint of ugliness or violence
Jarred amid the bee-invaded silence.
Doubts and dreads were spirited away
Earth was heaven on that timeless day.

Frances Barker

A Poet's Dream

Listen to the silence, of summer's gentle hush -
And peculiar to the mountain tops
Air perfumed by heather's brush.
And time stands still, in tranquil mood -
Enjoying sunshine's smile,
The quietness smooths ragged nerves -
And its peacefulness beguiles.
Inspired by such winsomeness -
The poet's pen runs free -
Expressing feelings from the heart -
Enchanting you and me
With images of nature's theme -
From that wondrous place of dreams.

Marian Curtis-Jones

A White Horse

Some dreams we remember, some fade from our mind
Some help us to reflect the deep meanings to find.

I was to go riding on a white horse one day
He came to me slowly to show me the way.

I wanted to fly and I wanted to run
But I leapt on his back to chase the sun.

He galloped so fast over rough dry terrain
Stretching before me was a wide empty plain.

My heart was thumping with joy at this sight
We rode for hours thro' the silent blue night.

The sunset from heaven, so red in the sky
Deep colours of purple shone deep in my eyes.

Where was I going on this wild lovely horse?
He was taking me to his own world, of course.

Jumping over banks and deep running streams
He had come to show me a place of my dreams.

I clung to his mane as the wind touched my heart
I cried when I awoke, as we had to part.

Wild was this stallion, as free as a bird
He took me to paradise but did not utter a word.

Janet Jeffrey

My Dream Place

Come with me to Florida
Feel the warmth of the sun as you go
Walk on the soft sand 'neath palm trees
And hear the breeze blow the leaves to and fro.

Search for beautiful seashells
Which litter the beach in small peaks
Watch the seabirds soaring and diving
Catching silver fish in their beaks.

Have a swim in the crystal clear water
Where dolphins play full of glee
Enjoying themselves as they put on their show
Riding the waves and leaping out of the sea.

Look out over the rippling sea
As the sunlight suddenly has to go
You will see the most beautiful sunset
With blazing sky and reflected glow.

A much calmer scene now takes over
As tranquil moon and stars shine so bright
Making long shadows from palm trees
We are bathed in her eerie light.

Most sounds of the daytime have disappeared
Except the light crunch of sand as we walk.
Waves lapping gently washing deserted beach
Fronds of the palms rustle slightly while we talk.

Betty R Lloyd

THE PLACE I LOVE

Sun-drenched sand,
Where ocean meets land.
Azure sea gently kissing golden grains,
Seagulls swooping whirl above.
Children running, laughing, splashing.
This is the place I love.

Angry face,
Clouds that race.
Screaming gale, whipping inky sea.
Raging waves towering above,
Roaring, crashing, tormenting sand.
This is the place I love.

Linda Townend

Perfect Peace

The gentle scent of meadow grass
and sunshine in a cloudless sky,
a distant lake that shines like glass,
fond memories as years go by.

Eyes shut, just listening to each sound,
each moment precious, gone so fast,
knowing there's beauty all around,
if times like this could only last.

Birds and bees, fragile butterflies,
fly and flit, their colours aglow,
shimmering as the heat starts to rise,
relaxed, at peace, no wish to go.

A tractor in the field beyond,
scattering grass ready for hay,
a lonely duck pecks at a frond,
playful squirrels head for their drey.

Myriad insects hurrying by,
carrying burdens twice their size,
wondering where they go and why
they manage with such enterprise.

Daylight fading, the sun sinks down,
shadows lengthen, dimming the light,
colours so vivid, now seem brown,
perfect day gone, welcome the night.

A Odger

On Holiday

We are on holiday sitting on the quay
The little boats are dancing on the water prettily
There is silence in the air, the birds are flying low
I'm sitting by the toilets 'cause I'm sure to want to go
All round the harbour the houses nestle in the hills
Up and up and up they go, this place is full up to the gills
Holiday flats at the back of us, high upon the heights
I bet the people in those flats can see amazing sights
Over there a hulk is sitting in the water looking kind of sad
I wonder where it's been to and the adventures it has had
It's only speculation but each picture tells a tale
I bet it looked magnificent when it was in full sail
But there it lies a'rotting on the water so serene
I bet when first that it was built it was fit for any queen
It is now a sad and sorry sight for anyone to see
I just can't help but wonder where its final resting place will be.

June Clare

Party Gossip

Oh he didn't?
Did he?

I couldn't have done?
No, tell me I didn't!

Did he really?
Oh what a fool!

The electric atmosphere,
All those alcoholic beverages,
Laughter at the games,
Flashing bright lights,
Thumping disco beats.

Mating ceremonies,
Sloppy, mushy corner scenes.

Oh they didn't?
Oh I didn't?
Did he!

In the light of day, I wish I hadn't!
Men think they can get away with it,
By just blaming it on the booze!
I hope us women can too!

Kim Rands

Of Such Stuff Are Heroes Made!

I often wonder what to do
to pass the time away;
to see the moments swiftly pass
to bring another day.
Today, I'm up and wondering -
at which I'm pretty good -
perhaps there's nothing extra 'spech' -
I don't feel in the mood.
The time will pass, I'm sure of that;
it hasn't failed me yet -
but up to now a longish sleep
is much the better bet.
I'm tired, I know, but Life is good.
We must enjoy it while we can
and a sleep for just an hour or two
builds an appetite for a man.
Don't waste my time, I've much on hand
to fill my day with rhyme.
One *must* keep going night and day
not to stultify the mind.

Andrew A Duncan

Beach People

Beach people, that is you and me
Enjoying the sun and the sea
Being lazy, getting a tan
Taking it easy for as long as we can
Slouched in a deckchair
Book in our hand
Come laze with us, down on the sand.

Feel, the summer sun beating down
A very slight breeze, is blowing around
Being barefoot, the sand tickles your toes
Children are laughing, having fun
As towards the water they run
Happy and carefree, watch them go
We are beach people, all this makes it so.

Look! It is a candyfloss van
Surrounded by kids young and old
All are excited, ready to hold
The pink, fluffy, sticky stuff
That is twirled, onto a stick
We prefer coffee, or perhaps
A nice pot of tea.
Either will be fine for you and me.

We built sandcastles
Collected seashells
Had a donkey ride
Took lots of photographs as well
Sadly, the sun is getting low
Time to pack up and go
It is really very tiring. Yawn! Yawn!
Being beach people, you know.

Nora McIntosh

PROMISES AND ROSE PETALS

Joyful news
From the village chapel
Childhood sweethearts
Have named the day,
Happiness all around
In the village square.
Village folk will 'lend a hand'
To make the wedding grand,
Flowers from their gardens
Will, in the chapel, stand
And dare we hope
Old Tom's prize roses
In the bride's posy
Buntings and streamers
All bright and gay
Will decorate the village hall
For this special day
Chapel bells will ring
Choirboys will sing
Hope the wedding morn,
Sunshine, bring.

Margaret Parnell

PREGNANCY

Having a baby, how lucky I am.
I could not imagine the joys to come.
Putting on weight, not able to sleep.
I must have counted millions of sheep.
Indigestion and pains here and there.
Anticipation, and of course what to wear.
Months go by, and clothes don't flatter.
Being like a balloon, getting fatter and fatter.
Woke in pain, and a whoosh of water.
Off to hospital for a son or daughter.
Push and pant, everyone shouts.
Don't they think I also want this baby out.
The waves of pain get stronger and stronger.
All this pushing and panting I can't go on much longer.
One big push, it's delivered with joy.
Congratulations Mum, you've got a lovely baby boy.

Anne Sackey

RING OF STONES

The ring of stones stand all alone,
high upon the windy moors,
relics from a time that's past,
guardians of the hidden doors.

Placed there long ago by druids,
users of forgotten lore,
there to watch that the unwary,
do not pass beyond the doors.

Passage ways to other places,
where the wild hunt still runs free,
to the land where magic courses,
through the grass and every tree.

Enter here the land of fairy,
where all things magic do abound,
once your through the hidden entrance,
the doorway back cannot be found.

And so the ring of stones stand guarding,
mortals from the secret doors,
keeping us safe from the magic,
hidden on the windy moors.

Jeffrey Kelly

PENNY LANE

Who took the road sign,
It should have been mine,
Does anything remain the same
In Penny Lane.
No time to stop at the barber's shop.
Will I remember to go to Sergeant Peppers?
It's just on the right.
Past the traffic lights.
This cafe was once the old toilets you know
Because of the tourists, it had to go.
No time to stop at the barber's shop,
I'll go and look through the charity shop
Window on the way,
Old ladies talk of yesterday,
It's cold beneath the blue suburban sky,
People busy shopping, rushing by,
Now I'm in a rush,
I'll catch the next bus,
Will I go home as before
Or will I embark a Magical Mystery Tour.

Isabel Taylor

JULIET CAPULET'S DEATH

She lay there with a chalky pallor,
with stiffened muscles and lips blue in colour,
she lay there with her blood running cold,
her chest lay still, never to bulge.

She was like an untamed flower,
which rose from the ground and did not cower.
But the untimely frost came abruptly,
and cut her down so murderously.

Emily Ruth Henderson (15)

A Little Lost For Words

Time seemingly expanded
That eventide - I remember so well
When a smiling moon
Cast her beam of light
O'er a water's surface,
Thus creating a magical circle
Of silver
          and
Within the circuit,
There did playfully jest
Displaying a talent,
Unique to his own - the Salmon!

A silent prayer,
I stood again - (Perhaps just)
A little lost for words!

Irene Gunnion

A Summer Storm

Come into the garden and listen with me
The birds are all silent perched in a tree
The air is still, and it is very warm
It must be the calm before the storm
Yes here come the clouds, so heavy and grey
It looks like a thunderstorms on the way
Big raindrops fall upon my head
I run for shelter to the garden shed
The lightning flashes the thunder rolls
The wind is gale force, it blows and blows,
The rain is heavy, it lashes down,
More thunder comes with a cracking sound
The river rises and bursts its banks,
There is a horse in the meadow, water up to its flanks
Branches are torn from many trees,
The ground is covered with twigs and leaves,
A thunder bolt hits the village hall,
The roof is gone beyond recall
It's like a river in the street, too much for the drains
A manhole cover is lifted, it rains and rains
But listen, the rain has stopped the wind has ceased
Once again there is quiet and peace
Look above the clouds have parted
The storm is over as quick as it started
Once more it is still and very warm
Now it's the calm after the storm.

Therese Spare

I Still See Your Face

I'm sorry that I hurt you,
Never meant to,
I'm sorry that I left you,
Didn't want to
But I hear you're doing fine now
Perhaps a little wild,
I still see your face each day,
When I look down at our child.

I'm sorry we didn't talk more
You didn't want to,
I'm sorry we didn't walk more,
Might have cleared our minds,
But I'm doing fine now,
No more days of acting wild
And I still see your face each day,
When I look down at our child.

Sandra Watton

WINTER IS . . .

Bleak skies that promise snow -
Goods they will not bestow.

Winter is . . .
When leaves' flesh rots in rain,
Till vein skeletons remain.

Winter is . . .
Doorsteps becoming slick with ice -
And rock-salt stolen in a trice.

Winter is . . .
Winds warning, with a whistle
That they're coming down our ginnel.

Winter is . . .
Drenched raincoats on a hall stand
Weather blustering like a brigand.

Gillian C Fisher

WHAT TO WEAR

What to wear, oh, what to wear
I search my wardrobe, tear my hair,
It's always such a trying task -
Does everybody have to ask?
Or do they choose - say
for today, I'll wear blue.

I lay the clothes out on the bed
contemplate what's best with red,
green or yellow, blue or pink?
Some help is needed, I can't think.

Try that with this, then this with that
but it's not right - I have no hat
to match the outfit. When it's cold,
and winter's here, so let's be bold.

I'll don attire of every hue
T'will brighten up the weather too.

In gay abandon I step out
in splendid colours. People shout,
look what she's wearing - how absurd,
the colour crazy, poor old bird.

Pam Dawkins

THE YOUNG JACKDAW

I'm not long from the nest. The thought of going solo,
getting airborne from the ground, sends little quavers fluttering
down my spine. My starboard wing feels stiff and crabby, awkward
as unworked hinge. Life weighs heavy, flat as sea-washed mud.
I lean against the garden wall, my soft grey pencil eye
not sharp enough to catch a shadow moving up the lawn.

Suddenly two sinewy hands fall from the summer sky,
and hold me tight as vultures claws. I screech like mad
and caw for mum, but no one answers. My fate is sealed.
Freedom ends inside the crowded darkness of a cardboard box,
where hope is squashed into a shaft of dusty light, a glimpse
of distant sky. I slump down on the floor and think of home.

The box is stuffy, not much air, not even room to shake a worm.
Nightmares come, a battery of metal cages occupied by rows
of squawking hens, banging their beaks against the bars; then
poor uncle Henry's rain-soaked carcass hanging from the gibbet
of a tree, and, worst of all, a grubby kitchen where a pastry cook
is stuffing three and twenty half-shot blackbirds in a tasteless pie.

This can't be real. I peck myself. My stomach churns. My legs
feel weak. I bang my head and beat both wings until they're worse
than black and blue. But then I think of dad. He wouldn't flap.
Stay calm, my child, he'd chirp, *and keep your pecker up.*
I settle down and listen to the rustle of the trees. At length
two voices break the spell with talk of predators and damaged wings.

The box is lifted high, the lid removed. I struggle free and stretch
my wings into the sky. Two anxious faces watch me swoop across
the lawn and soar above the trees, a world beyond the reach of cats.
I'm full of gratitude until a rain-soaked carcass swings before my eyes.
And then I want to rationalise, to understand. I shouldn't even try.
You just can't tell with God and humans, when and how, or why.

A K S Shaw

MEMORIES OF RUSSIA - 1917

You spoke of war, of revolution,
a family forced to flee its
home - refugees in their native
land - of Rostoff whose snow
clad streets silently awaited the
arrival of the Red Army - of the
boy standing by the window
anxiously listening for the
muted sound of horses hooves
advancing through the snow -
of rape, pillage and murder, three
endless days of piteous cries
before the perpetrators departed,
the civilised brigade arrived and
order was restored.

Jackie Hawke

THE BELLE OF THE BALL

She was the Belle of the Ball
And was so beloved by all.
Very young and ever so free,
Admired too totally was she,
Having no one there within call.

In passing she gave me the smile
I was waiting for all the while.
She was so happy and gentle,
But it was not accidental
That I was in no way her style.

He was sharp, gallant and dashing,
And appeared to her so smashing.
I just watched in all my sorrow
And wondered of her tomorrow.
Was it all to come down, crashing?

I decided to wait my chance;
In the distance to keep my stance.
She would later be tired of him,
For he might prove much too grim,
And then he'd lead a merry dance.

Thus, I needed to bide my time
For I was not now in my prime.
She knew full well I was present,
But chose not to show her consent -
I was obliged to wait some time.

After it all, she came to me,
Unbelievable as it could be.
She said she'd done what she should,
Knowing we each understood,
But it was me she wished to see.

Susan Audrey

THE TITANIC

It was really cold upon the deck
The night we hit the ice
Confusion all around us, panic and surprise
I thought of my friends down below
The tears filled my eyes
Then the shock, it struck me
I passed out for a while
In my semi-conscious state of mind
I wandered back in time
To memories, I had long since lost
I heard the voice, I saw the eyes
Take my hand said the stranger
As he looked into my eyes
Don't you feel the danger
Or do you want to die?
When I returned to consciousness
The stranger he was gone
I lay upon an upturned boat
Drifting all alone
Yet still at night I hear his voice
I see the stranger's eyes,
Maybe an angel that was sent
To save me from my plight
God rest all those who lost their lives
God bless them that survived
One day I will return to dust,
Until, we'll meet again.
Amen.

George Arden

A Wasted Life

I stood at the grave of my one time best friend
With whom I'd had many good times,
And thought it would be an idea if I penned
Just one or two relevant lines.

We'd been friends for years at the same school and sport,
He was better than I, racing bikes,
He'd take risks so often, without second thought,
As when riding o'er outcrops and dikes.

It just seemed to me that he lead a charmed life,
He achieved his success without care,
And when on the town with another man's wife,
Didn't mind if the world stopped to stare.

But all he had now is a plot six by three,
For a whole life of not caring tuppence,
Adultery and drinking, he thought would be free -
Perhaps Bill deserved his comeuppance!

Norman Brown

RUNAWAYS

A woman abused has no choice,
She suffers alone with no voice,
With little hope and beyond all emotion,
She walks away causing no commotion,
A bag in her hand for years of devotion.

Thrust into a world of which little is known,
With crying children hanging to clothing.
Sent to a place where time stands still,
Where everyone there has lost their will,
All crammed together with the same to say,
Everyone abused, all runaways.

Gina Millet-Rivera

A Soldier's Love Poem

They say that absence makes the heart grow fonder,
As I stand here all alone and cold,
I think of you my love,
You are the air that I breathe,
You are my strength that comforts me
Through these troubled times,
My heart dances with passion,
When I think of you.
Your soft voice wonders through my mind
And I long for the day that we will hold each other close
And our hearts can beat as one.
The loneliness I can bear,
For I know we will meet again
And the battle in my heart will be over
And peace will follow in my mind.

Sylvia Morrow

The Statue

Myriad's of colour thrown by cascading sunbeams
Upon two, still silent forms.
Combined with the warmth of crowds adulation,
Birth of a new life force.

Sculptured eyes, open for the first time,
Love that moulded their existence reborn.
Within marble depths, lifeless fingers flex,
Graze cool skin and consciousness dawns.

Imperceptibly, limbs draw closer,
Hearts bonded for eternity, pulsate.
Coils of delicate feeling, through systems unravel,
Altered figures by shadows, delineate.

Chosen by the artist for each other,
Modelled to survive the years.
Admired by all, for their form and beauty,
Entwined, safe from mere mortal fears.

Changed forever, in those sentient moments.
'The Lovers' discover the freedom of one.
Able at last to experience true emotion,
By the life giving strength of the sun.

Karen Davies

SKYLARK SONG

Skylark song
Echo across open field
Wild flowers
Dance with southerly breeze
Bees' legs
Covered in pollen
Hover from flower to flower
White powder puff clouds
Scattered across blue sky
Form images
Man on horseback
Dog running
Clouds drift apart
Different images appear
Nature ever changing art.

Mary Miller

Fluffy

For 14 years I had him
From kitten to old boy
My black four legged friend
Will be with me no more

He was not like your normal cat
He had a personality rare
He seemed to talk in his own way
To show you that he cared

He was always waiting for me
When I returned home at the end of the day
And he would run up to greet me and tell me it was time to play

But as the years rolled by his body gradually let him down
I tried all of the vets treatments and in the end I found
That it was kinder to let him go, painful as it was for me
Now he has gone away and lies resting by a tree

Buried in an orchard, beside another old furry friend
He had a lovely send off right to the very end
I never will forget him and I miss him greeting me
But his memory will live on just like the living tree

June Slater

SUNDAYS ARE SPECIAL

Very early Sunday morning
The farmyard cockerel loudly crows,
And wakes the vicar in the village
Who rises weary because he knows,
That today is not his day of rest
He must put on his working clothes.

First he dons his cassock
To hide his knobbly knees,
A snow white surplice around his shoulders
(His wife launders them in threes),
The finishing touch his clerical collar
Not so tight that it will squeeze.

Holy Communion starts the day
With broken bread and claret wine,
Then morning service where his sermon
Tells Saints and Sinners 'Toe the line',
To close the day comes evensong
Worshipping the Trinity divine.

His pastoral duties now complete
He homeward wends his way,
To sit down to dinner with his family
Then rest, meditate and pray,
A warm feeling of contentment
Brings to end his perfect day.

Bill Dovey

The Friday Walk

The walk was long and tiring
The sun was hot and fierce
The load I carried heavy
I thought my head would burst

If only I could stop a while
To have a cooling drink
My lips are parched, my throat is dry
But I haven't time to think!

Today I'm in a hurry
Today I've a job to do
No time to stop and think of it
I've a favour to do for you

As I trudge the dusty pathway
My thoughts begin to roam
My father is waiting for me
Saying 'Come my son, come home.'

It's not a job I relish
If I could forgo it I surely would
But I love my children dearly
So I really think I should

The sun is getting hotter
My lips are dry and sore
The cross I carry hurts my back
But the people cry for more

The blood runs down my forehead
From the thorns like knives I wear
Each step I take is agony
But this cross I *have* to bear

It won't be very long now
I've suffered the pain and grief
I am going to my Father's house
And there I will find relief.

And He said 'It is done'

A Taylor

THE PERFECT GIFT

She put the parcel David had given her
Down in her lap with the ribbon and pin.
What did it look like she thought?
David was purring with a silly grin.

This was a game they played every birthday
And Helen never grew tired of it
Nor did she ever make a correct guess
The packages were so made to fit.

Very carefully she undid paper number one
The parcel changed from an oblong to a square,
She had three guesses - so it is not a book.
She had undone the parcel without a tear.

Off came paper number two with a clue
'You know I'm not a rich man - but think big!'
Off came number three revealing a tiny box
'For the rest of the clues you'll have to dig.'

Helen was stunned. 'It can't be a ring!'
She said with a voice full of emotion:
'I dare not guess in case it vanishes.
You open it for me David - it's not a condition.'

With a flourish David opened the little box
And again there was a little packet inside.
Helen could bear the suspense no longer
She took the tiny packet and opened it wide.

David was humming 'Diamonds are forever.'
Helen put on the ring 'A girl's best friend'
And threw her arms around David's neck
'Wherever did you . . .'
But the thought was cut off by the end.

Rosemary Smith

Bygone Days Of The Past

Times of bygone days, ages past
Paths clad in snow, winter days, paths we walk
Horse-drawn cabs, Hackney cabs footprints in the snow
Carriage tracks, trees dressed in white
Gas lamps, streets, narrow paths.
Cloak covered gowns, knee length boots winter days
Smoking stacks.

People walking narrow streets
Coal-fired grates, smoking stacks, chimney sweeps.
Snow clad days, narrow streets we walk down,
Glowing embers, chestnuts toasting glowing brazier.
Carriage tracks, gas-lit lamps, snow covered hedges long
Cloaked gowns, knee length boots, top hats, fur covered coats
Walking sticks, ale houses, public bars
Open fireplaces, wooden beam, gas-lit lamps.

Snow clad days,
Chimney sweeps, smoke filled skies, grey skies,
Servant's quarters, attic rooms.
Times gone by, winter was long, Hackney cabs, people walking
Footprints in the snow, people talking
Carriage lamps, wheel tracks, footsteps in the snow,
Horse drawn carriages.

Gin sipping ladies, gas-lit lamps
Smoky rooms, snow covered streets,
Narrow passages; cobbled streets, ale drinking, pipe smoking
Gents smoky bars, open fires.
Top hat gents, long gowned cloak covered ladies.
Long gone ways, bygone days.
Snow covered streets, smoking stacks, gas lamps
Servant's quarters, attic rooms, long gone days.

A May

A Change Of Thought

Men in sturdy attire, ladies clothes so fine.
Old, thin pass-me-downs are mine.
Everyone moving nice and warm,
I've, nowhere to go and feeling forlorn.

People in carriages are going places
With cosy feet and rosy faces.
I, pray for shelter or a dorm
From, this snow and heavy storm.

Why did I choose to roam
Away, from siblings, and my home?
The work has gone, I don't belong.
Maybe, it's time I travelled on.

E C Hines

The Boulevard

The snow falls
And I lift my skirts, tiptoe across,
Looking neither to left nor to right
Lest I see what is no longer there.

The air chills
Even that minute spark in my heart
Which blazed bright like a furnace of flame
When the boulevard blossomed with spring.

A carriage
Overtook me just now on the road,
Muffled hoofbeats and wheels without sound,
Borne away, just as happiness flees.

Shapes pass me,
Unfocussed through my tear-blurred eyes,
Then dissolve into enshrouding mist,
Like the pale ghost of my lost true love.

Ivy Lee

ELEGANCE OF THOSE YESTERDAYS

Looking at a picture of times now past
and scenes of long ago
there is an essence of grace and elegance
that this world no longer knows.
And we have to admit that something is lost
that we can never know again
But we should not long for those yesterdays
. . . is it a longing in vain?

They did not have what we have today
like our luxuries of every kind
and for all of man's progress upon this earth,
we have so much that afflicts the mind.
So many knew only toil and pain
except the privileged gentry
but their elegance will never come again
It was the final graceful century.

A simpler world but so many more cared
And what they had they shared.

Irene Dalzell

Disturbing Perfection

Black marks embedded amongst white silk; Footprints in the snow.
Unplaced and gently pressed along the path; Footprints in the snow.
I think of where the people have been and which way is their home,
I stop and turn to trace my journey to see how far I've come.
Do I walk in peace or in vain for the viewing public; I do not know
My master guiding me with actions from the straps, I can't feel where to go.
Visually limited, restricted to feel no fear, instead I head for the horizon.
For hostile weather and deep curiosity scrambling my intentions.
Unable to feel the pull of the reigns or the lash of the whip, numbness through me.
Feeling nothing but perspective; the passing of people, tree after tree.
Serenading times lasting hold upon memories frozen in chaos,
I have been many places and strive for life drinking from a trough.
Waiting for those memories to melt, changing with the weather I know,
Just like those footprints being disturbed in the snow.

Adrian Dalzell

Picture Into Words

Looking and studying the picture it does tell me
That it could be the beginning of the nineteenth century.

It's winter time as thick snow lays on the ground,
It don't look busy as not many people are about town.

There are no cars like today only horse-drawn carriages
And most of the trees look bare, there are no leaves.

All the buildings stand tall with snow on their roofs
Imprints in the snow from feet, wheels and horses hooves.

Hands in his pockets some guy has forgotten his gloves
Looks like more snow, as it's dark and heavy up above.

Long dark coats looks like they could all be black,
In those days I think nearly everyone wore a hat.

It looks a peaceful time, people quietly going their way
No noise of cars, stereos, mobile phones, like we have today.

To step inside the picture that's where I'd like to be
Living in those days, that would have really suited me.

Linda Roberts

UNTITLED

For her the coldest season seemed to cover,
The pain created through losing a lover.
As the carriage pulled away
She turned to glance, turned to say
How much she yearned to be with him
Instead of whom she married.
Although he stood here with her now,
Although he promised, although he vowed,
She did not want to carry on,
To hide her sin, it was not gone
Among the snow and ice that day.
Inside, her passion burned away,
But he did not allow their love to bloom,
Disgrace like hers was sure to loom,
Over her marriage, over her life,
She cannot leave, she was his wife.
And when all was said and done,
They must believe the child's his son.

Claire Woolmore

THE HIDDEN WOMAN

Footprints lead away
from where the last fling plays to a closing notice,
on a boulevard so cold in breathless exhortations
he bartered trust with soothing reason;
our eyes aglow
tensions thundered across the snow - melt it will,
pain never melts away.
Deceptive patterns held
in frozen crystals of outward beauty,
and in our carefree hours unknown to me - faithful,
to a nook of three.
Muffled hooves and lifting chatter passing by,
and in their laughter a joyful spirit for me to muse
there once was I.
What more his ruinous eye would say
that dizzying passion had been rebuked, but my
flushed cheek was all of me;
vacant and edging and destiny calling not wanting
the trial of a stranger's look, we stepped aside
and I was free.

Tom Griffiths

Winter Wonderland

I recall when there was snow
The flakes fell down ever so slow
Faces pressed to the windowpane,
Bread from Heaven without a stain.

At night the moon shone, ever so bright
All the country, was gleaming white
Then in the morning, crisp and cold
There were lots of footprints to behold.

Children went out to play
To build a man, who would not stay
Frozen fingers, and frozen toes
Left slush and ice on the cobblestones.

Along came the beaming sun
Melted the lot spoiled the fun
We must wait till the north wind blows
Once again we'll have snow.

Mary Green

Winter's Day

The cold icy snow lays all around
Frozen and cold upon the ground
People trying to cross the road.
Carriages carrying a heavy load
The buildings stand dismal and grey
As people hurry on their way
There's no sun to brighten their day.
In long dresses and long overcoats
To block out the winter's chill
So they will not get ill.
Tall trees standing leafless and grey,
On this cold grey winter's day.

Trudie Sullivan

Cocooned

Dusk descended on the crisp snow,
Which glistened like icing on a Christmas cake,
Stinging winds now caught my face,
Catching my taffeta skirt
Which flapped and rustled
Around short boots,
Wedged firmly into frosty snow.
The usual clicking of the horses' hooves,
Now resonated a muffled solidity.
While comforting sounds of the carriages
As they rumbled past me,
Echoed long forgotten memories.
The security of my pram maybe!

Patricia Spencer

SUMMERTIME

Summer is here, fun time starts there,
Sandwiches on the front lawn, orange juice
and knickerbocker glory time.

Birds sing out their sweetest song
and pick up their bits and be gone.

I sit and admire the view
the flowers, trees and garden too.

The greenery is nice to see
as hubby cuts it finely.

I sip my ice tea by the golden ripe apple tree
and add a straw to my lips once more.

Cover up and settled down and have
forty winks on the ground.

I smell the mint and herbs growing nicely
by the sink
and the strawberries and raspberries that
are lovely and so very pink.

Yes, I love summer, every blessed hour
As I love and work hard for sure
the garden is looked after with
tenderness and much more.

A J Renyard

The Milliner

My leather boots are buttoned up and
warm out in the snow,
there is a young man I should know
how tall they seem to grow.

The pathway made by horses on their way
is the one that I must follow to my work today.

A tiny Milliners on the High Street,
is where I earn my living and buy my
nieces a treat.

They love the ribbons, laces, pretty hats,
and fancy ivory buttons shaped like tiny cats.

I work until the darkness closes in,
everyone works long hours to object
is thought a sin.

Jean Paisley

A Scene

Victorian times sealed the air
A gloom of winter set the mood
Pines so tall shed their wings
Were the women sad?
My guess is yes.
Styled in layer of cloth
Poised well.
It's clear as Hell
Gentleman of high rank
Stepped with confidence and wealth

Carolie Pemberton

Victorian Snow

The hardest winter I've ever known,
All the streets covered in snow.
Feet icy cold inside tight laced boots,
Long, warm coats on men in suits.
Trees so bare, lined in two rows,
No shelters for the birds to go.
Small peasant boys crouch on the floor
Near mounds of thrown snowballs galore.
Little girls bare footed in tattered rags
Hold lit matches near the bigger lads.
If only I could help these kids,
Whose life's been lived upon these streets.
Help get them safe out of this cold
Oh, if I could be so bold.
But a ladies place here is in the home
Not housing children from the snow.
To us we must stay in our place,
Beside our husbands to stay in grace.
Our voices, our words don't mean a thing,
The cold wind blows and our eyes sting.
We shed a tear for things we cannot change,
And then we just go on our way.

Anne-Marie Williamson

I Remember

When we were young
Life becomes a dream
As we step out together
Playing out life's childhood roles
I was the king and you were my queen
You were my life
My soul my best friend

As we face life's reality of tomorrow
No more dreaming
No more lies as we get a little older
We said our last goodbyes
Now as the years have passed us by
We meet once more
We talk, we laugh
About our boy-girl friendship
And our last long goodbye

Tony Jones

MEMORIES

It's pleasant to sit by the wave washed shore
And listen to the sound of the ocean's roar
With my own deep thoughts and nothing more.

How oft I have walked in days of yore
Holding my father's hand and he four score
By the sandy beach and heard his lore.

Now he's gone and I am old as I sit alone
By the rocky beach on his favourite stone
With pleasant memories, I have no moan.

Brigid O'Donnell

VIEW FROM MY WINDOW (MORNING AND EVENING)

No distant view greets my eyes in the morning
When waking from sleep green trees meet my gaze.
Birds blending their songs all chorused since dawning,
greeting the day with notes snatched from haze

Flowers blushing in well-tended border
colours mingling in rainbow-hued pride;
The gard'ner in charge keeps all in good order
allowing the weeds no safe place to hide.

Fine-pebbled footpaths make ways for our feet
to reach hidden places where many could go.
With here and there well-positioned, a seat,
giving a rest when resistance is low

When daylight fades the garden is resting
even the birds forget about nesting.

H Owens

In The Summertime?

Summertime surely brings out the best in us
Because there's a lot going for us.
The bright blue skies brightening the landscape
Inspiring the morale so promoting a confidence
As we're stepping it out.
And when outside, a cheeriness prevails
It seems everywhere and it's infectious,
Here we now have people in their
True colours because it's summertime.
Make the most of it while it lasts.

James Callaghan

THE PONY TRAP

I am the pony that is trotting by
Many years to go before I die.
The snow was cold, but I was well fed
My master was good
He gave me a fine bed!
Every day I earned my keep
Trotting up hills, some very steep.
I was blinkered and muzzled out there
Men and women paid for a fare.
When I retired, I rested each day,
I enjoyed the sun and rolled in the hay.

W L Jones

TICKETS

Hot summer nights to remember
Between the stairs, between the smiles
And the manager in the pub
Roams like a lion
Between drinks and basket chairs

The clock ticks on reality
And my voice is coming back
Funny how you miss simple pleasures
Deep feelings inside like a volcano
As exploding trumpets sound off
Beside Egyptian decorations

So summer nights lift off
To tell the truth of people out at night
And dancing feet relax
When the fun comes near
So the images roll like a film
And the past fades like sandwiches.

Kenneth Mood

THE ROYAL ACADEMY

He sits opposite me
In the restaurant
Of the Royal Academy.
His meal is a waste
For he does not taste,
Burying his head deep
His mind to feed
In a newspaper.
He looks around
Without having seen.
He pays his bill
Mechanical still
And now he leaves
Still in a dream.

M MacDonald-Murray

AUTUMN

The large red poppies have gone
and heavy clouds fill the sky.
The woods are still and silent
and September mists appear.
Secrets are taken to the earth,
as flowers begin to wilt and die.
The little folk hear these stories
when they come together at midnight.
Love is held in dark rich soil,
but never dulled by time.
The poppy seeds have scattered,
to fields we both once roamed.

Tom Clarke

A Voice In The Wilderness

Why has the world abandoned true values?
Where are we heading
At the end of the day?
Why are the principles
That some hold so dearly
Are watching them
Slowly swept away?
The spotlight is always
On pleasure and greed.
The children grow up
Without knowing true needs.
The pride of the Nation
Is being washed away.
The only source left
Is for people to pray.

Mary Tickle

ALL CHANGE

Some sit in comfort, most sit at ease
Others by size find it a squeeze
The start of a journey like making a nest
Shuffle the luggage ignore the rest
Then silence reigns like a gentlemen's club
Only the sound of the wheels as they rub
A table in front for papers or books
Passengers matching with almighty looks
While up in the corner a head is asleep
A solitary figure is having a weep
Then a human is heard saying something nice
Tensions are ended by breaking the ice
Heat fills the carriage and warmth starts to follow
Suddenly contact is all of a go
A countenance glows and loses its strain
This is the British when they travel by train
Refreshments announced as the train gathers speed
Specially worded so you can heed
Unisex toilets engaged for a while
Then long staying ladies emerge with a smile
The suburbs flash by for all to be seen
Then a voice that could end with God Save The Queen
'Your next station stop is coming up soon'
No cause to dawdle, time to make room
Then farewell from the Guard, a lady or male
This is the British when they travel by rail.

A Luke

THY HEART TO AWAKEN

Thou live in shame
Only thyself to blame
If thou doth believe
Thy life can feel free

Folk follow like sheep
And then to weep
Going hither and thither
Getting nowhere ever

If one but stay a second
There'd be time to reckon
That life can be supreme
With feelings serene

Thy heart to awaken
It is then
All else will follow
Bringing a life mellow

To be at ease
One feels a breeze
And thou will confess
There follows bless

To rise in the morn
At the break of dawn
Life feels a pleasure
For one to treasure

Go forward seek a good day
In every way
When nothing will blight
Your sheer delight

Josephine Foreman

How To Change The Weather

Driving in Italy we rowed
In our hot and overheated car.
Do we take the paying autoroute for speed
Or take the normal road that's cheap?

To my mind
The world does seem to hang
On single, simple threads like these -
For motorways you pay
And spiral materialism further high
You choke the air with gas
from slightly greater speed
You drive on straight and miss
the thought-enriching change of pace and scene
Poor world slips past a blue of fug
And we, in clockwork dream.

And why?
But for to reach the sun king's beach
an hour or something, sooner.
To sit 'neath sun,
And sleep, perchance to wither.
But this we did
And's how we changed the weather.

Decision made, my father frowned
And we became autoroute bound.
And so we did,
So, somewhere else,
The sun it went and hid
Behind some clouds.

Peter Stockton

Coda

The great performer took the stand,
The orchestra played frenziedly
Under the maestro's guiding hand,
His essay in modernity.

When it was over no one stirred:
Only after an endless pause
Was some appreciation heard,
A patter of restrained applause.

The genius could not meet their gaze,
His triumph under threat so soon;
Then someone spoke and lavished praise
On the finale's lovely tune.

The look in the composer's eyes,
That of a sinful soul reproved;
At much length he apologised
And promised it would be removed.

Christopher Brewer

The Third Anniversary

31st August 2000

On that Millennial occasion -
the third anniversary of the departure
of our magnificent and noble Queen of Hearts,
whose generosity of heart
made a mark on the 20th century at large,
thousands turned up,
from these towns and far beyond the shores.
They brought cheery cards
and countless flowers with a blaze of colours.
The fence of Kensington Palace
was smothered with them in no time.

Sweet fragrances wafted in the air around.
It was a wonderful spectacle by every account -
a visible testimony that she was honoured and loved,
even more than in her lifetime.

But after three days all the tributes vanished without a trace.
So the people were compelled to place
the new ones. Their intent
was to mark the anniversary of the final farewell
to our would-be - Queen Diana as well.

But when fresh posies of roses were being attached to the rails
of the Palace gate, for there is still no sign of her statue today,
two policemen appeared on the left and right,
as if we were committing some crime.

One of them, quite fat, coming from behind,
did demand an explanation why we did not celebrate
the life of Princess Anne.
In his version she had done more than anyone else.
Really, all were so taken aback, wondering should we laugh or cry.
Was he out of his mind? Princess Diana's sister-in-law did not die.

Lucy Carrington

A Winter Hazard

Snow reminds me of Canada,
Where it falls like powdery grain,
Freezing the air and the lakes,
Much too cold for rain.

Snowy apparitions,
Hang from the eaves,
Ghostly shapes, sit on trees,
Hanging on the leaves.

Glistening with jewel-like frost,
Roads are cleared in a trice,
People, clear their pathways,
Shifting snow but leaving ice!

'Go for a walk' they said,
'but be sure to wrap up warm
Just keep to the pathways
Then you won't come to harm!'

Setting out with trepidation,
I walked along the path,
Then reached a patch-uncleared
And promptly fell into a trough!

The more I struggled,
The deeper I sank!
Not a soul in sight
My mind went blank!

Oh! So cold, somewhat scared,
I thought I was a goner!
When a lady came by in a car,
Shouted 'Want help old timer?'

Thankful to be rescued,
I recorded it in rhyme!
It's funny to look back on,
But scary, at the time!

Evelyn Mary Eagle

DREAMS OF LOVE

Rooted to a golden sandy shore,
eyes searching an endless horizon,
hopes filled with fresh desires -
thus, each new morn I await
eagerly for your loving embrace.

Swells of your limitless passion
rise up from frozen depths and,
tantalisingly, your gentle fingers
touch my weathered face and
soothe my sun-scorched brow.

Your lips, soft as ephemeral foam,
I long to kiss and kiss and kiss,
but moon-made hands each tide
pull you relentlessly back, leaving
naught behind but your salty tears.

Over and over, I keep hearing you
call my name in whispers so
enticingly sweet - oh so sweet.
Yet, silent sorrow stills my voice
and pierces my stone-filled heart.

But in this lonely, wind-swept place
I will wait for thee to the end of
timeless time and until the moment
when the very rock of my soul melts
away into your enfolding arms.

E G Pryor

XMAS CARD FROM JTR

Your book's editor hoped everything you read here
Will look nice and soppy, and full of seasonal cheer
So prepare yourself for a bit of a shock my dear!
I've enclosed one of the most boring photos ever seen.
It's a typical bog-standard Victorian Christmas card scene.
It would be a different picture if the lady hadn't been
On time to take the Hansom Cab ride to escape from me again.
I once nearly caught her at the station but she got on a train.
I suppose it's for the best in the end, as it's really quite insane
To attack someone in broad daylight when it's been snowing.
It's best after dark when you sneak up without them knowing
And footprints might set events leading to my capture going.
I'm a good butcher. I do the best livers and kidneys you ever ate
While my photography skills are not yet all that great
So Merry Christmas from Jack the Ripper, for the year 1888.

Arthur Chappell